# Bear Grylls

## SURVIVAL SKILLS HANDBOOK

# SIGNALLING

# Bear Grylls

This survival handbook has been specially put together to help young adventurers just like you to stay safe in the wild. When you are out exploring, it's vital to learn how to signal for help in case of an emergency. If you are lost, injured, or the weather takes a turn for the worse, knowing how to use the resources around you to find help could be a life-saving skill. Once you have mastered these important skills, you're ready to start adventuring!

*Bear*

# CONTENTS

# GETTING STARTED

Signals are communication methods. They may work at close range or over quite long distances. Signalling is fun to learn and practise, but it's also a vital survival skill. In an emergency, it could save your life.

## Emergency signals

This book explores signals that are used by explorers, survival experts, and all who love the outdoors. Knowledge of signals allows you to call for help in an emergency. This could be vital if you are injured, lost, or trapped by bad weather, or survive a disaster such as a plane crash.

## Main types of signals

There are two main types of signals: visual signals that can be seen, and audio signals that can be heard. These correspond to the main human senses: sight and hearing. Visual signals include flashes, flags, hand and body signals, handwritten notes, and mobile texts. Audio signals include whistle blasts, phone calls, and radio transmissions.

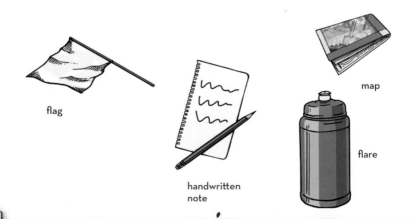

flag

handwritten
note

map

flare

## What to wear

Practise signalling outdoors in an open space. The right clothing and equipment are important on all outdoor trips and expeditions. Wear or take several layers of clothing so you can put on a layer if you are cold or take it off if hot. Take a cagoule in case of rain.

sunscreen

watch

gloves

food/drink

first aid pouch

sun hat

warm hat

walking boots
or shoes

**BEAR SAYS**

Before all expeditions, tell an adult where you are going and what time you expect to get back. If you are very late, the adult can then raise the alarm.

rucksack

compass

# SIGNALLING EQUIPMENT

You don't need a lot of fancy kit to learn the basics of signalling. Start with a few simple items and add more kit gradually as you need it. Some items are high-tech, while others can be made or improvised cheaply.

## Basic signalling kit

Many of these items are vital to wilderness survival generally. Carry them with you whenever you venture into the wild.

mobile phone

pouch

matches

torch

whistle

mirror

pencil

notebook

waterproof bags

marker pen

# Advanced signalling kit

Specialist items of signalling kit are also available.

survey tape can be used to mark trails

flint and steel can be used to light fires

flare (see page 26–27)

heliograph – a specialist signalling mirror

fluorescent marker panel can be used to send ground to air signals

radio transmitter (see page 40–41)

personal locator beacon (see page 40–41)

binoculars are useful for reading signals at a distance

satellite phones can be used to communicate from most locations

# GETTING NOTICED

Signalling is about getting noticed – sending messages that stand out in your environment. Distress signals are used in emergencies to alert rescuers that you need help.

## Attracting attention

The key to getting noticed is: Bigger, Brighter, Different.

Bigger – Humans are very small compared to the great outdoors. Make your signals large if you want to be noticed!

Brighter – Brightly coloured clothing, flashes, flares, fires, and loud sounds stand out in nature.

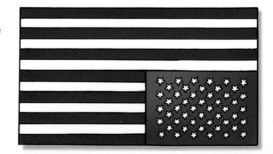

Different – Clothing and man-made objects with straight lines look out of place in nature. Anything that looks wrong, such as an upside-down flag or raised car boot, will also attract attention.

# DISTRESS SIGNALS

Distress signals are used to call for help in an emergency. Rescuers will risk their own lives to answer distress calls. These signals are taken very seriously, so should never be misused.

### SOS

SOS is an internationally recognized distress call. The letters stand for "Save Our Souls". Traditionally used by ships' captains, it is now used anywhere. SOS can be written as letters or sent as Morse code (see pages 22–23).

### Mayday

This distress call was originally used by airmen in trouble. Traditionally sent by radio, it comes from the French "*m'aidez*", meaning "help me". It is said three times.

### Three for danger

Any signal repeated three times is an internationally recognized distress call. This includes three blasts of a whistle, three light flashes, or three fires, arranged in a line or triangle.

## BEAR SAYS

If your distress call is not answered immediately, don't panic. It may take some time to attract attention. Wait about a minute between sending distress signals in a set of three.

# HAND SIGNALS

Hand signals are used by soldiers on manoeuvres. They are fun to use if you want to communicate silently with friends outdoors. Use them to move through a wood or open space without attracting attention.

Practise the signals with your friend first, to make sure both of you understand the gestures and how to give them clearly. You could also develop your own signs.

**BEAR SAYS**

Hand signals are useful when stalking wildlife to avoid frightening animals. Here you should give signals slowly - any sudden movements will spook wildlife.

## Movement hand signals

come here

hurry

stop                    obstacle

meet here

go here

wait

# Actions hand signals

listen

look

I don't understand

cover this area

I understand

breach

# Numbers

one

two

three

four

five

six

seven

eight

nine

ten

# USING NATURAL MATERIALS

Natural materials such as rocks, pebbles, and branches can be used to spell words and make visual signals. You can also draw letters in snow, mud, and sand.

## Choose your location

Picking the right location for your signal is important. It depends whether you want the signal to be seen from the air or from the ground.

### Good locations include:

1. A hilltop or ridge with an all-round view can be seen from the air and from all sides.
2. A signal on steeply sloping ground can be seen from below.
3. A clearing in a wood or forest is visible from the air.
4. An open grassy space can be seen from the air or higher ground.

## Gather materials

Decide on the materials to use, depending on what's to hand in the environment. You could use largish stones, branches, logs, or seaweed or pebbles on a beach. Carry materials to the chosen location.

## Prepare the ground

Clear the ground of debris such as stones that could distract attention or confuse the viewer.

## Scaling up

Make letters as large as possible, and at least three times as tall as they are wide. Letters should be at least 10 m tall, 3 m wide, and 3 m apart to be seen from the air.

### BEAR SAYS

If you move away from your signal location, leave an arrow to mark which way you have gone.

choose a patch of level or gently sloping ground

## Writing letters

You can trace letters with a stick in damp sand, mud, or snow. You can also tramp down snow with your feet, or shovel it away to expose dark soil beneath. On a beach, write a message above the high tide mark if you don't want it to wash away.

# SIGNALLING WITH COLOUR

Bright colours are great for attracting notice. In an emergency, a bright flag or garment can alert rescue services or even someone just passing by.

## Make a flag

You can improvise a flag from brightly coloured clothing, a space blanket, bivvy bag, or life jacket tied to a stick. Wave the flag above your head if help is in sight.

## Make a scarecrow

Make a cross of sticks and pull a T-shirt over it like a scarecrow. Remember: Bigger, Brighter, Different – this signal will really stand out.

## Tinsel tree

Shred a space blanket and tie the strips to a tree to signal in an emergency.

# BEAR SAYS

Once the emergency is over, be sure to erase all distress signals. Remember that rescuers will put their own lives in danger to save yours.

## Survey tape

Strips of survey tape can be tied to trees or bushes to attract attention or mark your route. You can write on this tape with marker pen.

## Dye marker

Some survival kits contain packets of dye marker. This coloured powder creates a clear signal if spread on water, and is also effective on snow and sand.

# SHAPES AND SHADOWS

Shapes, shadows, and silhouettes can be used to send visual symbols. Remember that straight lines and sharp angles stand out well in natural surroundings.

## Creating shadows

Shadows can be used to spell out letters when it's sunny. Create shadows by piling snow, sand, or earth into walls to form letters. The walls should be at least 0.3 m high, and will stand out even better if you dig a trench to make the wall.

You can also pile up branches or stones to form letters, but the letters will need to be very well defined for the shadows to be legible.

## Message cairns

Cairns can also be used to leave written messages. Place the note in a plastic bag, and leave it under the top stone of the cairn.

## Inuit cairns

In the Arctic, the Inuit traditionally build human-shaped cairns called inuksuit (singular: inuksuk) to mark trails and herd caribou.

## Silhouettes

An unusual outline silhouetted on a ridge will attract attention. Build a cairn of stones to attract notice or mark your route.

# BEAR SAYS

Your knowledge of distress calls could save someone's else's life if you notice an emergency signal no one else has seen.

walking in this direction

need equipment

need medical attention

need first aid supplies

## Marker panels

Some survival kits contain a marker panel. This is a large square of cloth or canvas with different colours on the front and back. The regular, man-made shape stands out in nature. Fold the cloth to send different signals as shown.

land here

do not land here

## Improvised marker panel

You may be able to improvise a marker panel using a tent and groundsheet or a bivvy bag and space blanket.

colour code

white

yellow

blue

# SEMAPHORE

Semaphore is a system of signalling using flags to spell letters and words. Semaphore was widely used by sailors in past centuries and is still used today.

### Improvise flags

Improvise flags with brightly coloured cloths or clothing. If you tie or sew the cloth to sticks, your signals will be clearer. Red and yellow stand out well at sea. Blue and white flags are clearly visible on land.

### Sending semaphore messages

Practise semaphore with a friend in an open space. Hold each position for at last six seconds. Count seconds by saying "one thousand and one, one thousand and two..." slowly. Then move to the next position, making the change obvious.

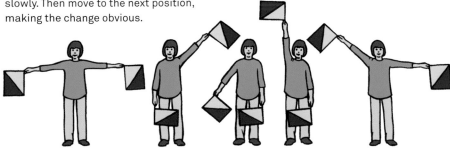

## Receiving messages

Binoculars can help you read signals over a distance. When receiving messages, draw the arm positions. Work out the letters and words after the signaller has stopped sending.

A     B     C

D     E     F     G     H

I     J

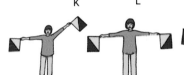

K     L     M     N     O     P

Q     R     S     T     U     V

W     X     Y     Z

cancel     numbers follow

## BEAR SAYS

Hold a flag in each hand with your arms out straight. There are eight possible positions for each arm.

19

# TRAIL SIGNS

Trail signs are used by scouts to mark routes and communicate with others following. In an emergency, trail signs show rescuers which way you headed if you moved on.

### Practise trail marking

Hone your survival skills with friends by taking turns to lay a trail and follow it. You can also develop your own signs, known only to your group.

## BEAR SAYS

Marking the trail is very useful if you are hiking in unfamiliar territory. On the way back, or if you lose your way, simply follow the markers to retrace your steps.

## Laying a trail

Each sign can be made using sticks, stones, or tufts of grass. You can also scratch signs in mud or sand. Leave trail markings at regular intervals, and at all junctions where followers will be unsure which way to go.

**this way**

**gone home**

**turn left/right**

**go straight on**

**message hidden (10) paces this way**

**not this way**

**water this way**

**message this way**

**message this way (over obstacle)**

**group split up**

# MORSE CODE

Morse code is an international code made up of short signals, or "dots", and longer signals, or "dashes". Developed in the 1830s, it is named after American inventor Samuel Morse, who invented the telegraph.

whistle

torch

## How Morse code works
Different combinations of dots and dashes represent numbers and letters of the alphabet. String letters together to make words and sentences.

Morse code messages can be sent using visual signals such as smoke, flags, and light flashes. Or you can use audio signals such as whistle blasts or beeps on a radio.

## Sending Morse code
Practise sending and receiving Morse code messages with a friend. When sending, keep messages short and simple. Write down the message and look up the code.
Send slowly, making signals as clear as possible. Pause slightly between each letter, with longer pauses between words.

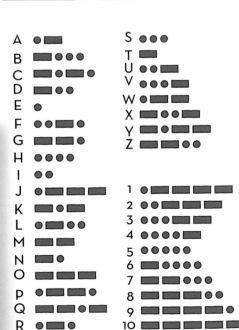

## Receiving

When receiving, write down the code for each letter. Work out the message when the signal stops.

## BEAR SAYS

SOS in Morse code is three dots, three dashes, and three more dots. Memorise this simple signal – in an emergency it could save your life.

## Morse code in flags

You can signal in Morse code using a flag or cloth tied to a stick. Hold the flag upright. Move it to the right for dots and to the left for dashes. Make dashes slightly longer than dots. To signal over a distance, move the flag in figures of eight to the right or left. Over a short distance these exaggerated movements aren't necessary

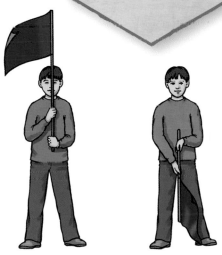

# MIRRORS

Mirrors reflect sunlight. You can use this to send light flashes that can be seen from a great distance. You can also use a mirror to signal in Morse code.

## Improvised mirrors

A hand mirror can be used to send a signal. If you don't have a mirror, many shiny objects will also reflect light.

tin foil

CD

tin cup or plate

glass shard

Practise sending and receiving Morse code messages with a friend using a hand mirror. It's not easy but, with practice, your technique will improve.

## BEAR SAYS

Keep moving the mirror slightly while aiming the flash at an aircraft, so you attract the pilot's attention without blinding him or her. Never signal an aircraft except in dire emergency.

## Signalling aircraft

In an emergency you can signal an aircraft using a mirror. This method takes little effort but only works when it's sunny.

1. Hold the mirror at shoulder height and point towards the sun.
2. Stretch your other arm out with two fingers up and palm facing inwards. Sight the aircraft (or another target) between your fingers.
3. Angle the mirror so a spot of reflected light hits your fingers.
4. Lower your outstretched hand while keeping the mirror at the same angle to direct the flash at the plane.

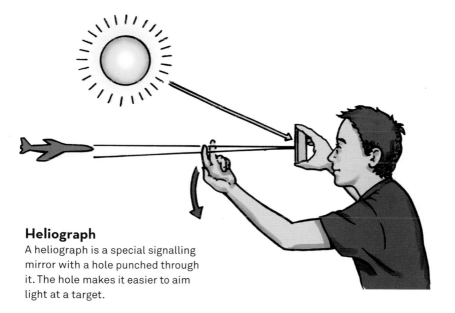

## Heliograph

A heliograph is a special signalling mirror with a hole punched through it. The hole makes it easier to aim light at a target.

## Using a heliograph

Hold the mirror up to your face and sight the aircraft through the hole. Your reflection shows a spot of light falling on your face. Tilt the mirror so the light spot disappears through the hole while you are looking at the aircraft.

# FLASHES AND FLARES

The signals described so far in this book mainly work in daylight. Torches can be used to signal in darkness, while flares can be seen by day or night.

### Improvised mirrors

Torches and flashlights can be switched on and off to attract notice or send Morse code signals. Strobe lights flash automatically to draw attention.

A torch taped to a branch and waved above your head sends a clear and obvious signal if rescue is in sight.

### Three for danger

Three torches flashed at once sends a clear distress signal.

### Whirling glowstick

A glowstick can be attached to a string and whirled to create a conspicuous circle of light.

### Conserve batteries

In an emergency, save torch batteries by signalling at intervals.

# Flares

Handheld flares produce a bright light or plume of coloured smoke that can be seen for miles. There are two main types: pistol flares and rocket flares. Warning: flares are very dangerous and need to be handled with great care.

## Handling flares

Keep flares dry and well away from a campfire. Remove one flare at a time from the box and replace the lid.

## Lighting a flare

Flares can get very hot so wear gloves if possible. Read all instructions carefully. Hold the flare out at arm's length. Point it at a 75° angle, not directly upwards, so burning debris does not fall on you or your camp. Follow the instructions to ignite the flare.

## ✗ BEAR SAYS

Position yourself in an open space that can be seen from all sides. Point the flare well away from anyone else. Brace yourself for the kickback when the flare ignites.

## Warning

Many flares are still burning when they hit the ground. Flaming debris can burn a hole in an inflatable life raft in a split-second. Avoid using flares in very dry areas where you could start a fire.

# SIGNAL FIRE

Fire and plumes of smoke are visible by day or night. For centuries, fire has been used to send signals, often in emergencies.

### Fire location

Choose a sheltered spot on level ground. If possible, make a platform of green (freshly cut, sap-filled) sticks or branches to keep the fire off the ground. You could arrange large logs or rocks around the fire to form a windbreak.

### Build a tepee fire

A tepee fire can be ignited quickly if rescue is in sight. Place a ball of tinder in the centre and pile kindling over it. Place small fuel sources over the kindling to form a pyramid shape.

## Methods of firelighting

The easiest way to light a fire is using matches, a lighter, or a flint and steel kit. Rub the steel along the flint to create a spark. If you have none of these, you can ignite tinder by focusing the sun's rays using a magnifying glass or even spectacles.

Blow gently on an ember to produce a flame. Add more fuel gradually, to avoid smothering the fire.

spectacles

flint and steel

matches

magnifying glass

lighter

## BEAR SAYS

Direct the spark or flame at the tinder. If it's windy, use your body as a windbreak, and cup your hands around the flame.

## Warning

Fire is very dangerous, so you need to be careful. Only light a fire with adult supervision. Have a bucket of water or sand handy to put out the fire if needed.

# BUILD A CONE FIRE

These techniques create signal fires that are clearly visible in open country or dense woodland.

## Cone fire

You need: green sticks or branches of various sizes, knife, string.

1. Sharpen one end of three long, straight sticks. Bind the blunt ends loosely with string, rope, or wire.
2. Fan out the sharpened ends to form a tripod shape. Push the sharpened ends into the ground.
3. Tie three shorter sticks about 15 cm from the base of the tripod to form a triangle.
4. Lay smaller, straight sticks onto the triangle to form a platform.
5. Build a tepee fire on the platform and place green branches over it. Leave a gap to ignite the tinder in the centre when you hear or see rescue coming.

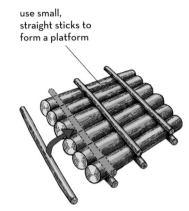

use small, straight sticks to form a platform

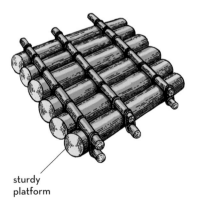

sturdy platform

completed cone fire

# SMOKE SIGNALS

A plume of smoke acts as a distress beacon. You can also send an SOS signal by fanning fire with a cloth.

Three fires in a line or triangle produce a clear distress signal.

## Fire raft

Dense forest or jungle hides fire and smoke. A river, pool, or lake provides an open space from where a fire will be visible, so the best place to site a signal fire is on a raft.

## Build a raft

Gather straight branches or bamboo poles. Lash them together crosswise, as shown, using string or rope. Tie the raft to both banks of a river and build a tepee fire on top.

## BEAR SAYS

Make sure any fire is completely extinguished before you move on. The smallest spark could start a destructive blaze, which could put you and others in danger.

# GROUND TO AIR CODE

Ground to air code is a method of signalling aircraft in an emergency. These signals can be made using natural materials.

### Gather materials

Rocks, branches, beach pebbles, or bright objects can all be used to make the symbols. You can also write the code in mud, sand, or snow.

Ground to air code is particularly useful as it makes it clear to aircraft if you need to be rescued, or if you need supplies to be dropped.

### Clearing a space

Choose open ground, a summit, or ridge top to site the signal. Clear away debris such as sticks and stones that could confuse the message. If using natural materials, make sure they stand out well against the background.

Make the symbols as large and clear as possible. These symbols should be five or six times as tall as they are wide.

## BEAR SAYS

The word FILL helps you to remember the three most important signals: food and water, injury, and all well.

require doctor
- serious injuries

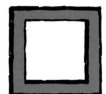

require compass
and map

all well

require medical
supplies

go this way

no

unable to
proceed

I am going
this way

yes

require food
and water

probably safe
to land here

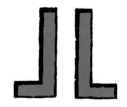

I don't
understand

# BODY SIGNALS

Body signals are also used to signal from the ground to aircraft. In an emergency, these signals can be used to guide a helicopter to a landing.

## Ground signals

In an emergency your first contact with the outside world is likely to be a search aircraft. Make this contact count by learning standard ground-to-air signals. You can use objects, as well as your own body, to seek help.

## Key
1. Need medical assistance
2. Use drop message
3. No
4. Yes
5. Do not attempt to land here
6. Land here
7. All OK, do not wait
8. Pick us up
9. Need mechanical help
10. Our receiver is operating
11. Wait, I can proceed shortly

## Prepare a helicopter landing zone

You need an open space at least 40 m across. The ground should be fairly flat and even. Remove debris such as rocks and branches, and also cardboard, paper, and plastic that could blow about.

**BEAR SAYS**

Exaggerate the body positions. Note that some positions are made side-on to the aircraft. Use a cloth to make the signals for "yes" and "no" clearer.

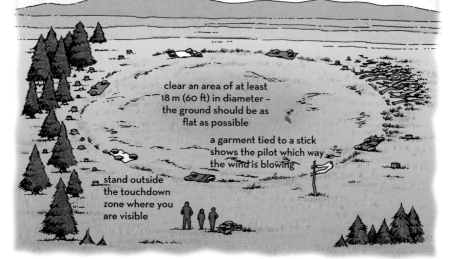

helicopter will approach downwind if possible

mark the edges of the touchdown area with bright items

clear an area of at least 18 m (60 ft) in diameter – the ground should be as flat as possible

a garment tied to a stick shows the pilot which way the wind is blowing

stand outside the touchdown zone where you are visible

## Warning

Beware of the helicopter blades and powerful downdraft. Approach the helicopter from the front, never from the rear.

# SIGNALLING WITH SOUND

The human voice doesn't carry far, and if you shout for a long time you will get hoarse. Noise-makers such as whistles and drums produce louder sounds that travel further.

## Objects that make noise

These objects are commonly used to create a sound signal.

banging two objects together

shouting

car horn

starter pistol

## Improvise

Improvise a drum by beating a hollow log or metal sheet with a stick. Or strike a metal cup or plate with a stick or spoon. Claves can be made with two dry, hardwood sticks. Strike one stick against the other to produce loud clicking sounds.

## BEAR SAYS

Whistles help members of a group keep in touch with one another, for example when moving through mist or woodland. You can work out your own signal code.

## Whistle

Blowing a whistle uses far less energy than shouting, and the sound carries further. Three or six blasts of a whistle is an emergency signal. Or send SOS in Morse code: three short, three long, and three short blasts.

## Grass squeaker

Put a blade of grass between your thumbs and knuckles as shown. Hold it taut, purse your lips, and blow between your thumbs.

## Wolf whistle

1. Stretch your lips over your teeth. Cover the teeth completely but keep lips relaxed.

2. Put two fingers between your lips as far as the first knuckle, with finger tips pointing towards the throat.

3. Flatten your tongue against the bottom of your mouth to within 1 cm of your gums.

4. Blow forcefully so air passes over your tongue and bottom lip through your fingers. Adjust position of lips and fingers until you produce a whistle.

# MAKE A WOODEN WHISTLE

Make your own whistle using elder wood or bamboo. Fun and easy to make and use, this could also save your life in an emergency.

## You need:

A knife, stick of bamboo or elder, or any wood with a central pith, thinner sticks.

1. Cut a straight length of elder or bamboo about the width of your finger.

2. Cut a finger-length section and remove the bark. Push out the central pith using a smaller stick.

3. Cut a 45°-angle notch about 2 cm from one end as shown.

**4.** Cut a length of straight stick slightly thicker than the central hole, and pare it down to make a dowel to fit inside.

**5.** Shave one side of the dowel slightly to make it flat. Insert it into the mouth end as far as the notch, so the flat side lines up with the notch. Trim off any end.

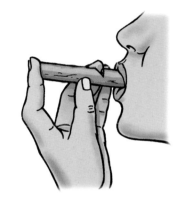

**6.** Test the whistle by blowing while blocking the far end with your finger. Adjust the dowel to alter the pitch.

**7.** Block up the far end using the dowel but without the flat side. This must be airtight.

# USING A RADIO

Radio provides an easy way to send and receive complex messages. Learn how to operate a radio before heading off into the wild.

## Radio equipment

Lightweight two-way walkie-talkies are an excellent way of communicating with a partner, a group, or base camp. If on an expedition, agree two specific times a day for transmitting messages.

## Getting a signal

Radio range is limited to within line of sight of a receiver. Reception is often poor in forests and cities. Climb to higher ground to get or improve a signal.

### Prepare to send a message

**1.** Raise the aerial but hold it level with the ground to get the best signal. Keep the aerial away from your body, clothing, or the ground.
**2.** Check if the microphone is activated by voice or button. Have the message ready and tune into the right frequency.

## BEAR SAYS

If reception is poor you can send an SOS in tones and beeps. The button may be labelled Key, CW, or Tone. SOS is three beeps, three tones, three beeps.

## Transmitting a message

Hold the microphone 10 cm from your mouth and speak slowly and clearly. In an emergency, say "Mayday, mayday". Give your name and position. State the nature of the emergency and the number of people. Then say "Over" and wait for the reply.

### International distress frequencies

VHF Radio: Channel 16
CB radio: Channel 9
Family Radio Service UHF: Channel 1
Amateur (ham) radio: 2182kHz, 14.300MHz, 14.313MHz
Airband Radio: 121.5MHz, 243MHz
UHF Radio (Australia): Channel 5

## PLBs

Personal Locator Beacons (PLBs) are small devices resembling handheld radios. In an emergency, activate the device to send a distress signal with your position to a satellite. This is then relayed via a ground station to a search and rescue centre which will send help.

# MOBILE PHONES

Mobile and satellite phones present the easiest form of communication – always provided you have a signal. It's also vital to conserve batteries or keep them charged.

## Mobiles and smartphones

Mobile (cell) phones allow you to call and text while on the move. If you are lost or injured you can take and send photos of locations or injuries. Smartphones provide access to the internet. You can download maps or a GPS app, which shows your exact location.

## Getting a signal

As with radios, mobiles only work in line of sight of a transmitter. They may not work in hills, canyons, or off the beaten track. Heading uphill may improve the signal. If the signal is weak, text rather than call.

## No signal?

If you have no signal but a full battery, send a text and keep the mobile on while you move on, the text will be sent if you enter an area with reception. If there's no signal and your battery is low, turn off and text from likely spots such as hilltops.

## Satellite phones

Satellite phones allow you to call and text from any location via satellites. Survival experts use them because they work in wilderness areas.

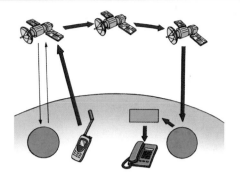

## Conserving batteries

Radios, mobiles, and satellite phones all rely on batteries, which need to be kept warm and dry. In icy weather keep them warm in a pouch next to your skin. Turn off devices when not in use, or buy a solar charger so you can charge your phone without electricity.

## International emergency numbers

Call these numbers only in true emergencies. Get ready to give your name, location, and the nature of the emergency.

| | |
|---|---|
| 911 | US, Canada, Mexico |
| 112 | Europe except UK, New Zealand, India |
| 999 | UK |
| 000 | Australia |

## Phonetic (spoken) alphabet

Use the phonetic alphabet to make sure any letters you use during phone calls or radio transmissions are understood.

| Letter | Code Word | Letter | Code Word |
|--------|-----------|--------|-----------|
| A | Alpha | N | November |
| B | Bravo | O | Oscar |
| C | Charlie | P | Papa |
| D | Delta | Q | Quebec |
| E | Echo | R | Romeo |
| F | Foxtrot | S | Sierra |
| G | Golf | T | Tango |
| H | Hotel | U | Uniform |
| I | India | V | Victor |
| J | Juliet | W | Whiskey |
| K | Kilo | X | X-ray |
| L | Lima | Y | Yankee |
| M | Mike | Z | Zulu |

## BEAR SAYS

Before going abroad, find out local emergency numbers and load them onto your mobile.

# SIGNALLING BY LOCATION

Different types of terrain suit various forms of communication. Here's a handy summary of what will work where.

## Open country and/or grassland

Visual signals such as flares, flags, flashes, and fire work well, particularly from hills and ridges. Phones and radios function well except in remote areas.

## Forest, woodland

Wooded areas are poor environments for signalling. Vegetation hides flashes, flags, and even fire and smoke, and blocks radio and phone signals. Don't ignite a fire or flare in a dry forest. Sounds such as shouts and whistle blasts are also masked by vegetation. Seek clearings, high ground, or open water to send signals.

## Desert

Open desert terrain suits visual signals – provided there is anyone to see them. Flags, flares, flashes, fire and smoke, and even written messages are easily spotted by aircraft. If lost or stranded, stay in the shade or by a broken-down vehicle, which will be conspicuous from the air.

## At sea

Marine areas have their own signalling methods. Lighthouses and buoys mark dangerous waters. Ships communicate using radio, satellite phones, lights, and flags. Use a light, whistle, flare, or dye to call for help from a small boat or in the water. Take great care when igniting flares. Helicopters will use a winch to rescue survivors.

## Mountains

Canyons and valleys block visual, radio, and telecom signals. Climb to ridges or summits above the treeline to signal using flashes, flares, flags, fire, or body signals. In mountain rescue code, six light flashes or whistle blasts signal an emergency. The response is three flashes or blasts.

## Polar regions

Visual signals work well here. Bright colours, manmade shapes, flares, fire, smoke, and dye stand out well against snow. Batteries and even whistles can freeze if not kept warm. Air rescue is likely to come from a plane with skids, not a helicopter.

# GLOSSARY

**Aerial** A metal rod used to transmit and receive radio signals.

**Audio** Relating to sound.

**Cairn** A pile of stones used to mark a route or summit in the wild.

**Claves** An instrument made of two hardwood sticks that are struck together.

**Conserve** To save or preserve something.

**Conspicuous** Something that is obvious or clear.

**Debris** Pieces of waste material.

**Distress signal** A call for help in an emergency.

**Environment** The surroundings, usually in the natural world.

**Green wood** Newly cut wood that is full of sap.

**Heliograph** A signalling mirror with a central hole that allows you to aim flashes of light at a target such as an aircraft.

**Ignite** To set on fire.

**Improvise** When you make something from materials that are to hand.

**Inuksuk** A human-shaped stone structure traditionally used by Inuit people to mark trails.

**Legible** Writing that can be easily read.

**Kindling**  Small fuel such as thin sticks, used to feed a newly lit fire.

**Marker panel**  A panel with different colours on the front and back, used for signalling.

**Mayday**  A traditional distress call. The word comes from the French "*m'aidez*" meaning "help me."

**Morse code**  A signalling system made up of long and short signals, also called dots and dashes. Morse code signals can be sent in different ways, for example by flashing a light or blowing a whistle.

**Personal Locator Beacon (PLB)**  A radio beacon used to send a distress signal and the sender's location in an emergency.

**Primary colours**  The three basic colours: red, yellow, and blue.

**Reception**  The receiving of radio signals.

**Semaphore**  A system of signalling using flags.

**Silhouette**  The dark shape of a person or object against a bright background such as the sky.

**Strobe light**  A torch or flashlight that flashes automatically.

**Tinder**  Very fine fuel used to catch a spark to light a fire.

**Transmission**  Something that is sent, for example by radio.

**Transmit**  To send

**Visible**  Something that can be seen.

**Visual**  Relating to sight.

# Discover more amazing books in the Bear Grylls series:

Perfect for young adventurers, the *Survival Skills* series accompanies an exciting range of colouring and activity books. Curious kids can also learn tips and tricks for almost any extreme situation in *Survival Camp*, and explore Earth in *Extreme Planet*.

Conceived by Weldon Owen, an imprint of Kings Road Publishing, in partnership with Bear Grylls Ventures

Produced by Weldon Owen, an imprint of Kings Road Publishing
Suite 3.08 The Plaza, 535 Kings Road,
London SW10 0SZ, UK

WELDON OWEN, AN IMPRINT OF KINGS ROAD PUBLISHING
Publisher  Donna Gregory
Designer  Shahid Mahmood
Editorial  Claire Philip, Susie Rae, Lydia Halliday
Contributor  Jen Green
Illustrator  Julian Baker
Cover image by  Emma Myrtle

Disclaimer
Weldon Owen and Bear Grylls take pride in doing our best to get the facts right in putting together the information in this book, but occasionally something slips past our beady eyes. Therefore we make no warranties about the accuracy or completeness of the information in the book and to the maximum extent permitted, we disclaim all liability. Wherever possible, we will endeavour to correct any errors of fact at reprint.

Kids – if you want to try any of the activities in this book, please ask your parents first! Parents – all outdoor activities carry some degree of risk and we recommend that anyone participating in these activities be aware of the risks involved and seek professional instruction and guidance. None of the health/medical information in this book is intended as a substitute for professional medical advice; always seek the advice of a qualified practitioner.

A WELDON OWEN PRODUCTION. AN IMPRINT OF KINGS ROAD PUBLISHING
PART OF THE BONNIER PUBLISHING GROUP.